Centennial Media Center
13200 Westlake Dr.
Broomfield, CO 80020

GOING TO SCHOOL
IN
COLONIAL AMERICA

by Shelley Swanson Sateren

Consultant: Melodie Andrews
Associate Professor of Early American History
Minnesota State University, Mankato

Blue Earth Books

an imprint of Capstone Press
Mankato, Minnesota

Blue Earth Books are published by Capstone Press
151 Good Counsel Drive, P.O. Box 669, Mankato, Minnesota 56002
http://www.capstone-press.com

Library of Congress Cataloging-in-Publication Data
Sateren, Shelley Swanson.
  Going to school in colonial America / by Shelley Swanson Sateren.
  p. cm.—(Going to school in history)
  Includes bibliographical references (p. 31) and index.
  ISBN 0-7368-0803-5
  1. Education—United States—History—18th century—Juvenile literature. 2. Schools—United States—History—18th century—Juvenile literature. [1. Education—History—18th century. 2. Schools—History—18th century.] I. Title. II. Series.
  LA206 .S27 2002
  370'.973'09033—dc21
                                                              00-011625

Summary: Discusses the school life of children who lived in the 13 colonies, including lessons, books, teachers, examinations, and special days. Includes activities and sidebars.

Editorial Credits
Editor: Rachel Koestler
Designer and Illustrator: Heather Kindseth
Product Planning Editor: Lois Wallentine
Photo Researchers: Heidi Schoof and Judy Winter

Photo Credits
North Wind Picture Archives, cover, 5, 11, 18, 25; Brown Brothers, 6; Stock Montage, 7, 21 (all); Bettmann/CORBIS, 3 (top), 12, 15; CORBIS, 27 (bottom); Historical Picture Archives/CORBIS, 19; Francis G. Mayer/CORBIS, 8, 9; 13; Archivo Iconografico, S.A./CORBIS, 27 (top); Lee Snider/CORBIS, 17; Colonial Williamsburg Foundation, 3 (bottom), 14, 22 (top); Archive Photos, 22 (bottom); Gregg Andersen, 23; Capstone Press/Gary Sundermeyer, 29

1 2 3 4 5 6 07 06 05 04 03 02

Contents

The American Colonies

In the 1600s, Europeans began building colonies in North America. Some colonists came to freely practice their religion. Other settlers made the journey to claim a piece of land and start a new life. Many people came to North America as indentured servants. Wealthy colonists paid indentured servants' passage. In exchange for passage, servants agreed to work for them for five to seven years. Many poor children also came to North America as indentured servants. Some children were stolen off London streets. This practice was called "kid nabbing." Strong and hard-working children usually worked as servants until adulthood.

American Indians had lived in North America for thousands of years. American Indian groups had built villages and cleared land for farming. At first, some American Indians welcomed newcomers and helped them survive in unfamiliar surroundings. Some American Indians shared their land with the colonists. Later, many colonists fought the American Indians and forced them off their land.

By the mid-1700s, thirteen British colonies had formed along the eastern coast of North America. Different climates and different ways of life separated these colonies into three regions—the New England Colonies, the Middle Colonies, and the Southern Colonies.

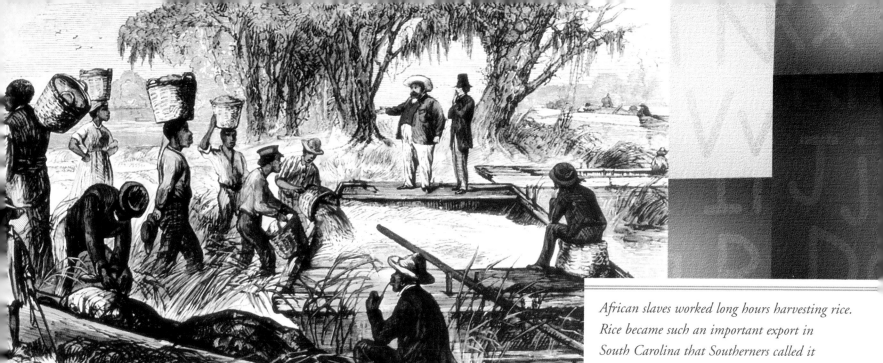

African slaves worked long hours harvesting rice. Rice became such an important export in South Carolina that Southerners called it "Carolina gold."

The New England Colonies were densely populated. Many colonists lived near towns and cities. Most New England colonists were farmers, shop owners, or tradesmen.

People who lived in the Middle Colonies farmed large fields of grains. The Middle Colonies, which supplied all British colonies with grains for breads, became known as the bread basket.

In the Southern Colonies, most people lived in rural areas. Most southern colonists owned small farms. But some colonists lived on large plantations. Plantations were self-sufficient communities that had farm buildings, churches, cemeteries, and blacksmith shops.

Plantations depended on African slave labor to farm large fields of tobacco, rice, and indigo. Until the early 1800s, slave traders took people from West Africa and sold them to plantation owners. Many plantation owners mistreated their slaves. They forced slaves to work long hours, six days a week. Some plantation owners beat slaves who complained. Many African families were separated when plantation owners sold slaves to other plantation owners.

Most colonial families did hard farmwork and chores every day. Children helped with planting and harvesting crops. In colonial times, many household items needed to be made by hand. Colonists made their own soap, candles, dishes, and furniture. Many children helped with these chores. Children also gathered food and hunted. Colonists spun their own thread to sew clothes. Girls learned to spin at about age 6. Young girls learned to knit as soon as they could hold a pair of knitting needles.

England ruled the 13 American colonies. In the mid-1700s, English officials began passing

Colonial girls learned to sew and knit at a young age. Children helped their families with many household chores.

General George Washington (on horseback) led the Colonial Army during the Revolutionary War. He later became the first president of the United States of America.

laws that put taxes on many goods brought into the colonies. Colonists did not want to pay the taxes because the taxes were set by the British government instead of their own colonial government. The colonists began to talk about forming their own country.

King George III did not want to give up the American colonies. He sent soldiers to enforce English laws. Colonists formed their own army to fight the English soldiers. These actions began the Revolutionary War (1775–1783).

With many fathers gone at war, families had extra work at home. Many families farmed. Family members worked together to plant and harvest crops. Children helped with extra chores, such as feeding the farm animals and tending the garden.

Many children did not attend school during the Revolutionary War. Their schoolmasters often joined the Colonial Army and many schools had to close until the war was over. Women sometimes taught students while schoolmasters were away at battle.

In 1783, the British Army retreated, and the war ended. The colonists gained their independence. Leaders from the 13 colonies named their new country the United States of America.

Women sometimes worked as teachers while schoolmasters fought in the Revolutionary War.

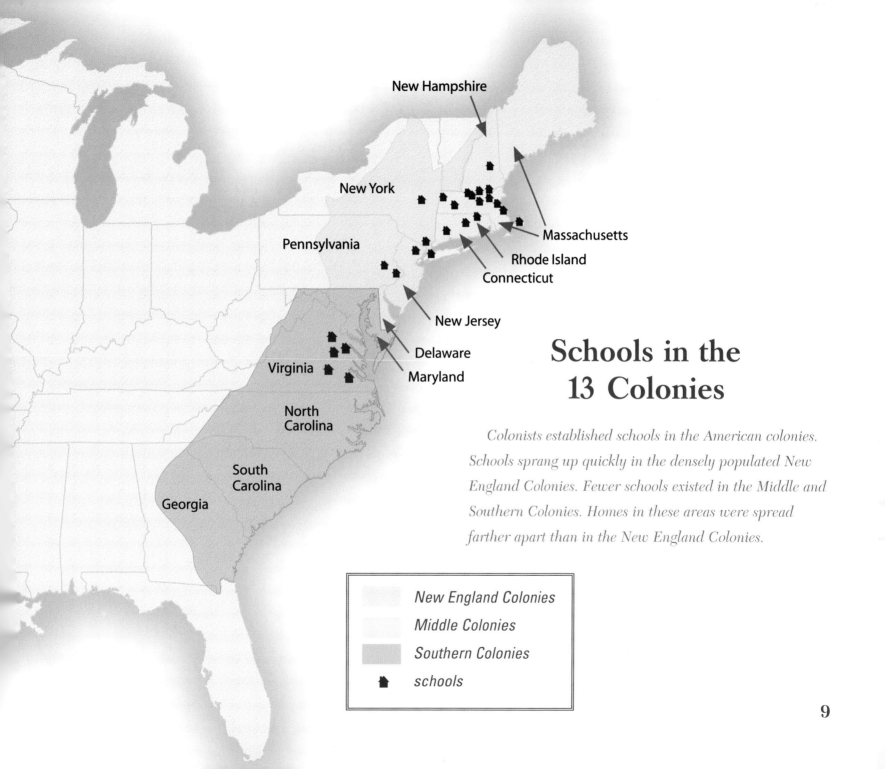

New Hampshire

New York

Pennsylvania

Massachusetts

Rhode Island

Connecticut

New Jersey

Delaware

Virginia

Maryland

North
Carolina

South
Carolina

Georgia

Schools in the
13 Colonies

*Colonists established schools in the American colonies.
Schools sprang up quickly in the densely populated New
England Colonies. Fewer schools existed in the Middle and
Southern Colonies. Homes in these areas were spread
farther apart than in the New England Colonies.*

New England Colonies

Middle Colonies

Southern Colonies

schools

Schooling in the Colonies

In the 1600s, most colonial parents wanted their children to receive a basic education. They wanted their children to learn to read and to study the Bible. But few schools existed in North America in the early 1600s. Many families lived in rural areas, far from towns and schools. They did not have any form of transportation to send their children to school. Many children learned to read and write at home.

Missionaries set up many of the first schools in the colonies. They wanted to teach people about Christianity. In the mid-1600s, New England colonists built several American Indian schools. Missionaries worked at these schools teaching American Indians how to read and study the Bible. African slaves were not allowed to go to school. But some Africans were free. Missionaries ran Sabboth schools for free African Americans. They gave lessons about the Bible.

As towns grew, colonists built more schools. Most schools opened in thickly populated New England towns. In 1647, the General Court of Massachusetts passed a new school law. Every township of at least 50 homeowners was required to hire a teacher to teach the town children to read and write. Because townspeople lived close together, most children walked to school. Many children who lived on nearby farms walked 3 to 4 miles (5 to 6 kilometers) to get to the village schoolhouse.

Town governments expected parents to teach their children basic subjects. For this reason, many towns built grammar schools where children who already had these basic skills could begin preparing for college. Grammar schools offered classes in geography, spelling, reading, English grammar, and Latin.

By the late 1600s, the New England Colonies had more schools than any other region in America. New England became known for the high quality of its schools. New Englanders were very religious. They wanted all children to be able to read and study the Bible. Most New England schools taught the three Rs—reading, writing, and arithmetic.

After the Revolutionary War, New Englanders set up city, or district, schools run by town governments. Many district schools

Schoolmasters taught students of many ages in one classroom. In some towns, boys and girls went to school only a few months a year.

did not receive enough money to stay open for more than a few months at a time.

Few schools existed in the Middle Colonies. A religious group called the Quakers settled in this region. Quakers believed in a practical education. In 1689, William Penn opened Friends Public

School in Philadelphia. Penn wanted all children to be taught a useful trade or skill starting at the age of 12. He believed this kind of education would create useful and successful townspeople. Quakers opened many private schools where boys learned sea navigation, bookkeeping, and surveying. For girls, teachers offered classes in needlework and other crafts.

Many children from New England and the Middle Colonies became apprentices. They lived with tradesmen for three or four years, learning their job. Tradesmen set rules for apprentices and punished them if they disobeyed or misbehaved. During apprenticeships,

Colonial children sometimes went to "dame schools." Women taught young students the alphabet and basic reading skills in these primary classes.

children also learned how to read, write, and cipher, or do arithmetic. Some boys became apprentices when they were as young as 6 years old. Colonists offered apprenticeships for blacksmiths, carpenters, painters, shipbuilders, metalworkers, ropemakers, and sailmakers. Girls received apprenticeships in needlework, sewing, spinning, weaving, and other crafts. Some girls apprenticed as cooks, bakers, pastry makers, and sellers of prepared food.

In the Southern Colonies, farms and plantations were spread far apart. Most parents instructed their children at home in the evenings. Many Southerners wanted more schools to be available for children. Plantation owners sometimes donated land and money for the development of schools.

For some rural children, old field schools offered a basic education. These one-room schoolhouses stood on unused farmland. Itinerant schoolmasters sometimes taught in rural areas. These men continually traveled throughout a region, teaching children in one old field school for a short while and then moving on to teach at another school.

In colonial times, girls made samplers to show their sewing skills. This sampler is from 1786.

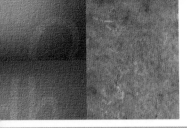

Plantation children often attended school in small classroom buildings located on the plantation.

Some wealthy plantation owners sent their children to England for an education. Others hired European tutors to teach their children. Several plantation owners sometimes hired a tutor together to teach all their children.

Colonial women taught girls the responsibilities of running a household. Girls needed to know how to cook, sew, garden, and efficiently finish daily chores. Most girls in the American colonies did not receive an education beyond basic reading and writing. Some schools allowed girls to attend classes in the evenings or during summer. In the late 1700s, some colonial parents sent their daughters to private finishing schools. Finishing school teachers taught needlework, music, art, and manners.

Plantation owners' wives taught their daughters how to manage many household duties and plan work for slaves. Plantation girls also learned how to plan large meals and supervise chores such as hog killing, meat smoking, and cooking. Private tutors sometimes instructed southern girls in music and dance.

Colonial Schoolmasters

In colonial times, most schoolmasters were men. Most of these teachers were about 16 years old. Some schoolmasters were farmers who held school during the winter months.

Some colonial women held "dame schools" for young children. Children gathered in the woman's home and learned basic reading and writing skills. Women sometimes held classes for older girls, teaching them reading, arithmetic, manners, Latin, and French.

Some southern children took lessons from circuit-riding parsons. These local pastors traveled from home to home, teaching children from their congregations.

Colonial schoolmasters did not make much money. Teachers sometimes boarded around with families. They stayed with one family for a week or two, then lived with a different family for a while. In this way, they received room and board instead of a salary. Because many colonial families were large, classrooms sometimes were crowded. One schoolmaster often taught 40 or more students of different ages.

Colonial schoolmasters prepared quill pens before school each morning.

The Colonial Schoolhouse

Most New England schoolhouses in colonial times were one-room, clapboard buildings. Colonists filled gaps between boards with a clay and grass mixture called chinking. Five or six small windows with 8 to 12 panes each lined the side walls to provide light for the students. Some schoolhouses were painted red or yellow.

Schoolhouses had a large fireplace at one end of the room. In some New England Colonies, parents helped pay for their children's education by supplying firewood for the schoolhouse. If parents forgot to send firewood to school, their children often had to sit in the seats farthest from the fireplace.

Colonial schoolhouses had a raised platform near the fireplace for the schoolmaster's desk. Sloping shelves lined the side walls and served as writing platforms. Children faced the platforms, sitting on long, backless wooden benches. Students kept their books on a shelf beneath the desk slope. Some schoolhouses had double desks. Two children sat at each desk. Desks often had a hole cut into them to hold an ink jar.

Some colonists who had large families built schoolhouses next to their homes. They hired tutors to teach their children.

The first schoolhouses in the Middle Colonies were log structures. These schools sometimes had a floor made of split, smoothed logs. Around the room, colonists stuck sticks into the walls. They nailed boards to the sticks to use as desktops. In colonial times, glass was expensive. Many schoolhouses in the Middle Colonies hung greased paper in the windows instead of glass. The lard made the paper transparent to allow light into the schoolroom.

17

In the Southern Colonies, schools often were abandoned livestock barns or sheds. Even plantation owners' children attended schools in crude, unfurnished structures.

Most colonial schoolhouses had a schoolyard. At mid-morning, the schoolmaster said, "You may go out." Students went outside for a short recess. During recess, children played marbles, tag, or hoops. When recess was over, the schoolmaster tapped the doorpost with a flat, rulerlike stick, called a ferule.

Schoolmasters kept a fire burning in the fireplace throughout the school day.

Whipping Posts and Whispering Sticks

During the 1600s and 1700s, schoolmasters were strict. They expected students to perform their recitations well, pay attention during lessons, and behave in a respectful manner. Schoolmasters punished students for disruptions and mistakes.

Many colonial schools had a whipping post outside the building. Schoolmasters tied misbehaving children to the post and hit them with a leather strap or a wicker stick, called a rattan.

In the classroom, teachers often quieted children with whispering sticks. Schoolmasters made students who were caught whispering hold these wooden sticks in their mouths. Whispering sticks sometimes had strings attached to the ends to tie in back of children's heads. Other schoolmasters pinched students' noses with slit sticks. Students kept the sticks on their noses until the schoolmaster took them off.

Some New England schoolmasters made children wear a dunce cap if they did not learn their lessons. Teachers made students wear these tall, cone-shaped hats and sit on a stool separated from the rest of the class.

Schoolmasters sometimes punished unruly students by tying them to a whipping post (bottom) and whipping them with a wooden stick (top). Some whipping posts had leather straps.

A Colonial School Day

Schoolmasters separated colonial students into several classes. They grouped children according to the level of their skills. Each class consisted of children of different ages. Boys and girls usually attended separate schools.

In grammar schools, colonial students read from the Bible and from primers. The colonial school day began with a Testament, or Bible reading, from one class. Students took turns reading from the Bible. Each student stood while reading.

In colonial times, books were rare and expensive. Students were careful with their books. They often used thumb papers to protect the pages. Students folded these small pieces of newspaper or wrapping paper around the pages where their thumbs held the book. Students also used tweezer-like tools called page turners to turn the pages. Thumb papers and page turners kept students' fingers from soiling the pages.

Many colonial children studied from the *New England Primer*. The early Primer was a book of short devotions, the Lord's Prayer, the creeds, the Ten Commandments, and a few psalms. The book covers were made from thin pieces of oak, covered with a coarse, blue paper. Other primers included short religious and moral stories. In the late 1700s, colonists began printing many of their own books in the United States.

Young children studied from hornbooks. These wooden study boards were shaped like paddles. Hornbooks had a piece of paper attached to the paddle, printed with the ABCs, the Lord's Prayer, a reading lesson, and a few simple sentences. The paper was covered with a thin, clear sheet of cow hoof, called horn. This covering protected the paper. Some hornbooks had cords strung through the handles so children could hang them around their necks.

Many young students also studied with battledores. These two- to three-page illustrated primers contained a short sentence for each letter of the alphabet. A battledore had a folded flap that secured the pages.

Some students owned revolving alphabets made from two wooden disks, about 5 inches (13 centimeters) wide. A piece of paper was between the disks. One side of the paper had

Colonial students used hornbooks to learn to read (below). The New England Primer *used moral lessons to teach children the alphabet (left).*

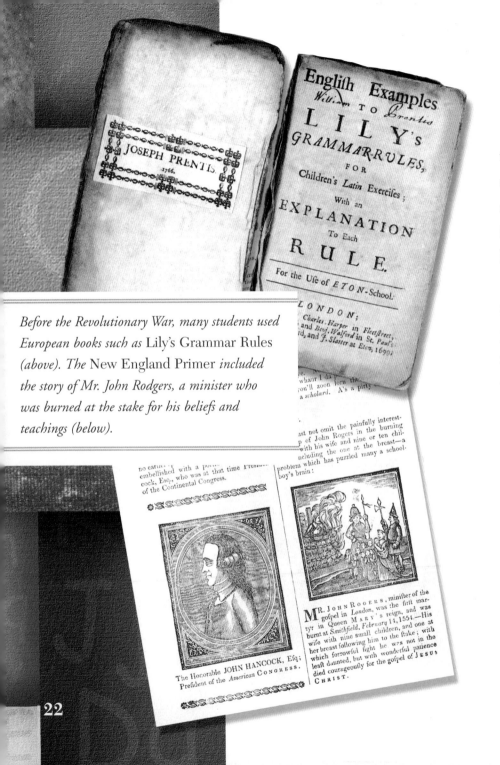

Before the Revolutionary War, many students used European books such as Lily's Grammar Rules *(above). The* New England Primer *included the story of Mr. John Rodgers, a minister who was burned at the stake for his beliefs and teachings (below).*

the alphabet. The other side had a series of syllables. A small opening was cut near the outer edge of each disk. By turning a thumb piece, the paper revolved between the disks, revealing letters and syllables in the opening.

In colonial schools, penmanship was an important subject. Writing time began by preparing pens and ink. During winter, ink often froze in the inkpots. Students thawed and watered the ink to thin it. The schoolmaster made quill pens by cutting the ends off goose quills at an angle. Children dipped the pointed end of the quill into the inkpot. The quill did not hold much ink. After several letters, students needed to dip the pen again.

In the 1600s and 1700s, paper was expensive. Schoolmasters seldom gave students paper to use. School paper was rough, dark, and unruled.

Make a Quill Pen and Berry Ink

Colonial schoolteachers had to be good pen makers and pen menders. The shaping of feathers into pens required fine skills. It often took the teacher two hours each day to make and mend enough pens for the whole class.

What You Need for the Quill Pen

1 long bird feather (you can find feathers at most craft stores and hobby shops)

a sharp knife or a scissors

What You Need for the Berry Ink

medium bowl
liquid measuring cup
1/2 cup (125 mL) frozen raspberries or blueberries, thawed
potato masher
strainer
small bowl

measuring spoons
1/2 teaspoon (2 mL) salt
1/2 teaspoon (2 mL) vinegar
1/8 cup (25 mL) water
small mixing spoon
small glass jar with lid, such as a baby food jar

What You Do to Make the Quill Pen

1. With an adult's help, cut the quill at a slant using the knife or scissors. The quill is hollow. This hollow area holds the ink.
2. Dip the pointed tip into your ink.
3. After you use the pen for a while, the point will become dull. Mend the pen by trimming the end.

What You Do to Make the Berry Ink

1. In the medium-sized bowl, mash the berries with the potato masher.
2. Set the strainer over the small bowl. Pour the berry liquid through the strainer. The juice will drip into the small bowl and the strainer will hold the berry pulp.
3. Add salt, vinegar, and water to the berry juice. Stir.
4. Over a sink, slowly pour the juice mixture into the jar.
5. Dip a homemade quill pen into your ink to write on paper.
6. Tightly seal the jar with the lid when finished.

"I went to the winter school . . . kept by Lewis Olmstead—a man who made a business of ploughing, mowing, carting manure, etc., in the summer, and of teaching school in the winter. He was a celebrity in ciphering, and Squire Seymour declared that he was the greatest "arithmeticker" in Fairfield County. There was not a grammar, a geography, or a history of any kind in the school. Reading, writing, and arithmetic were the only things taught . . . not wholly from the stupidity of the teacher, but because he had forty scholars, and the custom of the age required no more than he performed."

—Samuel G. Goodrich, Ridgefield, Connecticut, late 1700s, from Old-time Schools and Schoolbooks

Paper came in foolscap size, about 13 inches by 16 inches (33 centimeters by 41 centimeters). Students often folded the large paper to make four to eight pages. Because paper was seldom used, children often wrote on strips of birch bark instead.

Students often learned to write from copybooks. These books contained sentences that encouraged kind and respectful behavior. By copying the sentences, children improved their handwriting and learned how to behave well.

In the afternoon, students gave their recitations. Students recited, or spoke, homework lessons from their readers every day. During recitations, children "toed the crack." They stood in a straight line with the toes of their shoes touching the edge of one of the floorboards.

Many grammar schools also taught students arithmetic, or ciphering. Most colonial children did not own their own printed arithmetic books.

Early arithmetic books, such as *The Schoolmaster's Assistant*, were printed for schoolmasters to consult.

Some New England schools taught history, geography, and Latin. Many history books were religious. In 1708, an illustrated history book was published. It was titled *The History of Genesis*, after the first book of the Bible.

Other books also existed for school-age children. One of the earliest elementary books published was *The Child's Weeks-work*. This textbook contained daily lessons for four weeks. The book included proverbs and fables, which taught children lessons on morals and behavior. In addition to these lessons, *The Child's Weeks-work* had a prayer section and a catechism, which children used to learn the teachings of the Bible.

During recitations, students lined up and "toed the crack" along a floorboard. The schoolmaster asked students questions about their lessons.

Exhibition Day

The most exciting day for colonial schoolchildren was exhibition day. Schoolmasters held this event at the end of the term. On exhibition day, students showed parents and townspeople what they had learned during the school year.

Before exhibition day, students prepared writing samples. Instead of writing copybooks, students displayed penmanship by writing an exhibition piece. They wrote these short essays on happiness, friendship, obedience, and kindness.

Students displayed their work on exhibition day. They placed their writing samples out on desks for others to see. Children often recited short essays or Bible passages in front of parents and townspeople. On exhibition day, teachers sometimes quizzed students through oral examinations. Teachers asked students questions, and they answered them out loud.

Schoolmasters also held public "spells" on exhibition day. During a spell, schoolmasters gave children words to spell out loud. The schoolmaster often selected words from *The London Spelling Book* or Webster's *The American Spelling Book*. Students toed the crack and took turns spelling words. Students who misspelled their words took their seats. The student left standing at the end was the winner.

Students carefully prepared writing samples to display on exhibition day (left). Colonists held public whippings to discourage townspeople from committing crimes. Students sometimes were dismissed from school to attend these events (below).

Colonial students had special days off of school. In the New England Colonies, schoolchildren had a day off to watch criminals be publicly punished. Criminals often were placed in stocks. Theses wooden devices locked the criminals' hands and feet. Criminals stayed in stocks for a set number of hours, depending on the crime. Colonists hoped public punishments would stop other colonists from committing crimes.

Noah Webster's Spelling Book

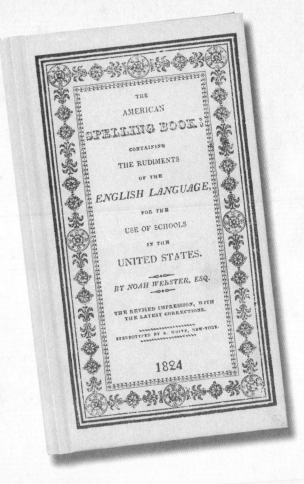

In colonial times, people did not have set rules for spelling. Many colonists spelled the same word in different ways. They often spelled words the way that they sounded. For example, colonists might spell "young" as *yong* or *yonge*. They sometimes spelled "himself" as *him self* or *himselfe*. In the late 1700s, Noah Webster wrote a spelling book to create a more simple and unified system of spelling.

Webster eventually named his spelling book *The American Spelling Book*. Throughout his life, Webster expanded and improved his spelling book. Many people referred to Webster's spelling book as "The Old Blue-back." After the Revolutionary War, Webster's blue-back speller became the main textbook for many students. Webster's spelling books became the main dictionaries in the colonies and were expanded to the dictionaries used today.

Have a Spell

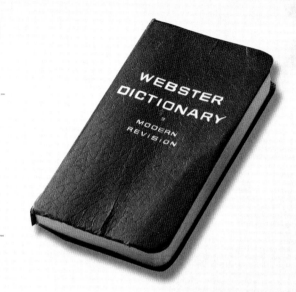

What You Need

a dictionary

paper

pen or pencil

one player to be the leader

four or more players to be spellers

What You Do

1. The leader picks six easy words from the dictionary and writes them on the paper. The leader picks six harder words and writes them below the easy ones. The leader then picks six difficult words and adds them to the bottom of the list.

2. The spellers must not look at the words on the paper. Spellers should "toe the crack," or stand side-by-side in a straight line. The leader calls out a word and the first speller in line tries to spell it correctly.

3. Students who misspell their words sit down. Students who spell their words correctly remain standing for their next turn to spell.

4. Continue the spell, looking up additional words in the dictionary if necessary.

5. Keep playing until one person remains. The final player standing wins the spell.

Words to Know

apprentice (uh-PREN-tiss)—a person who learns a particular trade or profession by working and living with a skilled tradesman

catechism (KAT-uh-kism)—a book or section of religious teachings and questions for studying

chinking (CHINGK-ing)—a mixture of mud and grass used to fill gaps between wall boards

cipher (SYE-fur)—to figure or to do arithmetic

climate (KLYE-mit)—the typical weather in a geographical region

fable (FAY-buhl)—a story that teaches moral lessons

itinerant (eye-TIN-ur-uhnt)—traveling from place to place

proverb (PROV-urb)—a short saying that teaches a truth

spin (SPIN)—to make thread by twisting together thin fibers; colonists spun thread on wooden spinning wheels.

survey (SUR-vay)—to measure an area of land to make a map

To Learn More

Barrett, Tracy. *Growing Up in Colonial America.* Brookfield, Conn.: Millbrook Press, 1995.

Carlson, Laurie. *Colonial Kids: An Activity Guide to Life in the New World.* Chicago: Chicago Review Press, 1997.

Dosier, Susan. *Colonial Cooking.* Exploring History through Simple Recipes. Mankato, Minn.: Blue Earth Books, 2000.

King, David C. *Colonial Days: Discover the Past with Fun Projects, Games, Activities, and Recipes.* American Kids in History. New York: John Wiley & Sons, 1998.

Wister, Sally. Edited by Megan O'Hara. *A Colonial Quaker Girl: The Diary of Sally Wister, 1777-1778.* Diaries, Letters, and Memoirs. Mankato, Minn.: Blue Earth Books, 2000.

Internet Sites

Colonial Williamsburg
http://www.history.org

Jamestown Settlement and Yorktown Victory Center
http://www.historyisfun.org

Plimoth Plantation
http://www.plimoth.org/museum/museum.htm

Schooling, Education, and Literacy in Colonial America
http://alumni.cc.gettysburg.edu/~s330558/schooling.html

Places to Visit

Colonial National Historical Park
Route 17 & Goosely Road
Yorktown, VA 23690-0210

Colonial Williamsburg Foundation
310 South England Street
P.O. Box 1776
Williamsburg, VA 23187-1776

Jamestown Settlement
Route 31 South at Colonial Parkway
P.O. Box 1607
Williamsburg, VA 23187-1607

Plimoth Plantation
137 Warren Avenue
Plymouth, MA 02360-2436

Index